OKAY COOL NO SMOKING LOVE PONY

OKAY
COOL
NO
SMOKING
LOVE
PONY

Annik Adey-Babinski

THE WORD WORKS
Washington, D.C.

THE WORD WORKS
P.O. Box 42164
Washington, D.C. 20015
editor@wordworksbooks.org

Cover art: Sue Montoya,
"0.0," 2016, Print.
Cover design: Susan Pearce Design.
Author photograph: Gesi Schilling,
courtesy of Jai-Alai Books, Miami, Florida.

LCCN: 2016962787
ISBN: 978-1-585-16-7

ACKNOWLEDGMENTS

Many thanks to the editors who published versions of the following poems:

Best New Poets 2014: "Wash Bucket"
Cosmonaut's Avenue: "Breaking and Entering"
Fjords Review: "Monster" and "Bull Among the Narcissi"
Forklift, Ohio: "I Wanted to Find America" and "Selfies"
Moose and Pussy: "Wildwife"
Prelude: "October, Miami"
The Puritan: "On MC Hammer's Birthday"
Salamander: "Miami As Lover"
Sink Review: "Munchausen by Proxy"
Ten Cent Journal: "How to Get the Ghost Out of the Pool"
Transom Journal: "March Storm"

The following poems appeared in a Jai-Alai Books anthology, *Eight Miami Poets*, in 2015: "Breaking and Entering," "Munchausen by Proxy," "Broken Air Conditioner Poems," "October, Miami," and "Surprising Animals." Thanks to P. Scott Cunningham for including them.

I am grateful to Denise Duhamel, Campbell McGrath, Les Standiford, Florida International University's MFA in Creative Writing program, the Knight Foundation's John S. and James L. Knight Fellowship, The Banff Center's 2011-2012 Wired Writing Program, Chloe Garcia Roberts, Nancy White and The Word Works, and my families.

CONTENTS

For Michael and Tina

WASH BUCKET

He
showered with a small sick bird. They stood
together under the barn roof, out there,
bathing in
watery tracechains,

man and bird lathered
silly in
velvet froth,

the blue wings just
blue. No one stopped

the water. By
now we all knew a
man like that was best left to his great
acts. Goofy
medicine, we'd learned, worked. A calmness
came over the farm. He
turned off the water and whinnied

at the morning. He was once
a man who slept in bar bathrooms &
felt nothing. Then
we don't know what happened to the

man. The farm was quiet. The whole
field empty. He was somewhere beautiful,

we hoped. He came back blue-black
and started to give good advice. From the sky

we'd fallen into this world and when we fell
we broke. That was why, he said, climbing on
the main beam of the barn, clamping his
hands around the wood, we loved—to try to get back.

SQUALOR

Most of
us learned to live like a bootleg,
in the open corners, our presence overpowered

by
shadows from the
purple smell

of kerosene. It was the colors of
our kitchens—forest collards,
pumpkin soup & pink catfish—

that kept their attention &
taught us that everything could be candied—
counter tops, kisses, sinks & yams.

RITUAL UNION

No more can I return to this
moment
      I could
fill the small black car
leave the blinds properly
shut
and drive north.
I am forbidden
      from repeating these exits.

Goodbye to that bad habit.

Goodbye to stranger days

      when I could kiss
in dance's sweaty oblivion
another searching mouth.

Goodbye to all
that I've left behind already
but now decidedly leave.

It feels less like
taking off a burden
than I thought it might.

Is it supposed to be heavier?

We've run through
without each other before.

Goodbye Montreal.
You were good
and cruel to me.
You ruined me.

Goodbye friends on the roof.

Do I have to say goodbye to it all?
Do you want proof
        I won't return?
Because I might
and I could.

Whose will is working now?
With all of these finalities?
With this tragic bow
to the performance of youth?

It feels heavier going forward
than the idea of me
in the car.

I hear some decisions
feel right
immediately.

Gathered
under a tent
or under the open sky.

Goodbye open nights
waiting for bells and calls.
Waiting for someone
who could put words
in the right shape.

Who could hold me
with those words
and watch me struggle.

Goodbye, goodbye,
old life spent
longing for this.
I feel I might cry
both kinds of tears.

MONSTER

the local childlover let the runaways
stay with him
but i wouldn't sit on his lap.
i already knew about that
power, that giving should take a cost.
out in the chicken coop
he'd find eggs about to hatch.
birds just starting to peck out their walls.
he'd hold the shaking stone
in his hand and break back
the dented shell, the milky tent,
staring down as the half-born chicks
drowned in his palm.
i've known
the winter and chose it over
that sunken house. chose to be lost.
a small lean-to
against a pine.   until they find it
i get the vein and sleep through the day,
spend the nights staying warm
in trucks by the lake.
my belief we return
to hurt each other grew
and when the cars pulled away
i drew a circle in the gravel
with my shoe. i would stand in the circle
until i didn't feel my toes
then i'd wake them on the long trail home.

I WANTED TO FIND AMERICA

Driving long alone,
this first rest stop after the border
like an epiphany. The woman inside
sells me another phone card.
She is kind and calls me *Hon'*.
Road signs look more sure of themselves here,
so I load back into the car, feeling very fast.
It's raining hard in the mountains
and my wiper is broken.
My car keeps shaking on the downhills.
Think of dying in a different country.
Pray to god, the one on the money.
It's overcast and I'm driving by a river
where men are fishing
up to their knees in freedom.
I want to try that fish. I want
to buy a root beer and an Archie Comic.
I want to own a keychain covered in stars.

THEY FOUND THE BOY

drinking Mr. Patterson's pool water.
The boy was covered in hair
and howled like a wolf
so we think he came down
from the yellow mountain.
The snows had started,
the peak was gray
and cloudy.
The first birds
landing on the treeline
shook off the snow
in nervous lines
across the hill.
The boy came out
of those lines.
A golden streak
bright out of the mountain's green vein.
He was thirsty.
There was a bolt of lightning
in his head that told him to do things.
The light in his head told him
everything was personal—the weather
the bird on the tree, the car's lights—
all messages from a god
that did not exist.
He ran through the streets
hitting cars and cats and his own head.
Snow had descended on the town.
Men got caught
in the storm under their cars
on rolling wooden slats

with metal rusting in their hands
the salt water from their eyes streaming down
just pouring into the street.
The town shed tears
Yes, we want to cry with you
we told the boy
but he'd left no trace
in the newly minted snow.

BULL AMONG THE NARCISSI

He stood alone in my backyard, among the narcissi
bowing, hidden at the hedge. His black sides heaving.
Breath so faint he murdered language,

blind from the halo of stars on his neck.
Narcissi swayed against his chest
and the lavender crocus heads healed in the night.

As I said before, he suffered such attacks. The little flocks
quaked at his feet, the wet cedars marked his back.
And the bull blinked. Not a response, but a rest.

LITTLE FUGUE STATE: CAT BATH

When you leave,
the old story says,
you bring with you
what it was you fled.

In this way, a riverhead
gurgles, fountainous and dumb
under the amber bathroom lamp.
Overflowing with words you know.
Lime dip ringing the bath.

Into the tub with you,
yellow night, sorrow,
and sulfurous terror.

A drowned sleep!
A new, resistant strain!
Interrogate the bed.

Now that you mention it,
dark, scratching thing on the wall,
your panic is familiar.
Flutter, flutter, skit.

She climbs against the tiled room,
thin and yellow with lime
and the deepest earth.
She is not here. She left
through the spigot, and the drain,
but first floated unsteady at the ceiling light
and ashed on us below, who had lost
even a meow to hold against her.

ON MC HAMMER'S BIRTHDAY

This morning went out to North Miami more
95 than I'd like in a day Eddie told me
he remembered the bike I was talking about
found the right mirrors streamlined deco things
to match her red and white paint job

later listening to "Can't Touch This"
we'll wonder what the new Pope would say
about celibacy outside the church
we decide he wouldn't
believe us Kelsie tells me
she spoke to her long-distance Boo
for two hours "That's Wowza"
remembering he's crossed the country twice

we love us
swooning on the beach yelling
boys' names into the sea
and calling eyes scrambled eggs
I still believe in snail mail
but can't survive on stamp glue send me a picture
taken from your street and I'll step into it

BROKEN AIR CONDITIONER POEMS

Black birds with big beaks picking at the godhead bodily
Wrapped in golden sheets they arrived in the godhead bodily
Singing in the dark they spoke of the godhead bodily
Wrung in cherry bark they boiled from the godhead bodily

Eleven wings and other things broken from the godhead bodily
Wilt by now the homegrown flower grown of the godhead bodily
Little bones and broken teeth crushed in the godhead bodily
Burning moths fluttered in the cloth dying at the godhead bodily

Big wings and I showed them king
Convinced it was medicine, I called it king
Three grey palms and they called him king
The end of September and they called him king

Kitty on the ledge and I knew it king
That was how it tricked me, called me king
Little plastic music maker, made me king
Singing to the seraphim I spelled out king

So the seventh angel sounded, wounded lambs and marks on doors
So the seventh angel sounded, raising bees from grass in swarms
So the seventh angel sounded, like untimely figs the stars did fall
So the seventh angel sounded, harped off the night in silver calls
So the seventh angel sounded, swept golden locusts from the rails
So the seventh angel sounded, lay together with stings in our tails
So the seventh angel sounded, while we rose from the sand anew
So the seventh angel sounded, the sun burned black, night askew

HEPATITIS

I hear the bells again
—of virus—
of cold air in the blood.

We know what happens.
There is no vaccine for this.

I hold the honey
in my hand.
You asleep with a dog
at your feet.
I wonder how much longer.
The night cools off your heavy eyes,
the heat in my jaw
unquenchable.

Stop saying things.
Stop putting your blood on me.

DOMESTIC DISTURBANCE

Wrecking
sleep, the crews

of men
railed on walls, unable
to hold the women, to
understand catch
and release. The females sparrows,
the men without
gentle nets. Breaking
things, clipping wings,
they fell into
the windows, splinters
flew around the sill. We heard blues-horn

calls for mercy.
Bloodlines.

THEY TOOK THEIR TIME

to
come inside, scattering pigeons,
leaving us cooing
in
our rooms, hanging from the eaves
hoping not to be seen. Silent as
black
cats, mouths full of feathers,

we seemed to float
over the sounds on
the first floor, to
hear them as blueprints.
Our minds sparking
like fireworks in empty lots.

THE OTTAWA VALLEY

We Valley People are uncanny folk.
Something in our twangy talk, the slack magic
of our bog boots, the way we work, hoodooed,
through the swampy winters, divides us
from the rest. We swim in logging rivers till
October, waist-deep in yellow leaves, then step into the
dark months. When the snow melts, the men hunt varmints
and the women lie out on dried blacktop in bikinis. I didn't
think it was true, when I learned my cousins could taste
a coming fog. They taught me it was like sour metal, bitter
at their molars. I could follow the stars to the Great River or
trap a muskrat in its hole for dinner. I knew how to summon the wild.

There would be no speaking of this. It was taken as good
& left alone. Other magic visited our lives with
regularity, familiar as our momma sharpening her knives.
New hop shoots, the fresh corn we
boiled in vinegar for winter. We believed
the green waste water, pooling in the sink as we
drained the cast iron, could keep away night wolves, & we weren't
going to test faith, dancing like strung-up varmint, wild & poor.

IS THIS WHAT THEY MEAN
WHEN THEY SAY IT'S WORK?

In your absence
I make myself a grilled cheese
the way you would for me if I asked.
Burn the bread reading on the couch
with your cat kneading my belly.
This is my silent apology because
I told you I would not apologize
for anything and in your maddening way
you grew calm and rational.
I eat the buttered, blackened bread,
glory, glory, carcinomy, and in my
sorry mind I tell myself it's Sunday,
it's midday, it's alright to lie in bed
as I have been, and find comfort only
in the rhythmic circling of the ceiling fan.
You may come home, greeting
the queenly cat and pulling open
a bag of chips, noting my undone
dishes in the sink, my still-closed door.
Or you may not, and I will feel a relief
that what I've been both fighting against and
working for at last is. I will sit on the back porch
and tend to my plants. The lovely winter
lost on them, I'll note it in their place.

OCTOBER, MIAMI

Since I've moved to America
I find myself more often thinking
I'd like to be rich
but what I mean is
I'd like to feel safe I'd like to relax
I know it's not my business
but when you wake me up
at 3 AM yelling at the cops
and again at 5 AM banging
on your apartment door downstairs
and when under my window
I hear your girlfriend
ask you where her daughter is
and why you've been watching
porn with the four-year-old
I start to wonder if it isn't
because I've had a few beers
I can relax about the yelling
downstairs and the door slamming
repeatedly but then there's still
the cockroaches on the stove
the sink the counter the walls
the bathroom my toothbrush
the utensils the plates and cups
in the fridge on the cutting board
I burn them when I can
but mostly now I ignore them
like the sounds below
I try not to think about living
in this mean city
it is a hard life here if you aren't rich
knowing most everyone else

lives month to month
mouth to mouth we resuscitate each other
working nights without childcare
hoping your gas doesn't run out
knowing it's a bad sign
the whole building smells
like mold and there is that leak
from the bathroom above
held in only by the many layers
of paint when I poke the wall
it bounces like a balloon
no doubt driving the roaches
insane in my shirts in my books
in my bags in my shoes
termites leaving their jewel-peppered wings
piled in my underwear drawer
their waste on the windowsill
the one that dented so easily
because it had been eaten from inside
like you
treating your daughter cartoon-like
beating her mother
while the building cowers
behind locks at your rage
I imagine you'll shoot us dead
in our beds or burn the whole
place in the early morning
how easy it would be
I thought I might try it too
I thought we'd only leave
a small smudge on the concrete
like salt rust on the bottom of a car

SORTILEGE

Sometimes in the bath
I have my flame and I have the heat
In the glass beside me
The heat being fearsome
Holding the water spice
Against the inside of my lips
No Meekie don't come in
I dropped the alcohol in the bath
Oh love
A bath takes me
A bit to the brokenness
Nothing like this lying in heat
This surrender
The weight of rest in bathing
The heaviness here in the water
No more in me
No more sharp in my ears
No more water at the glass
Heat still in the jar by the bath
Winter rising in the air
Can we still drink from the same glass
If I can't have your blood in mine?

CONTROL POEM

Fill the room
With light and action
And make it unavailable
For other uses

The fast animal in the bathroom
Dies in a lemon spray
With your heart in its chest
Stopped beating by now
You wish its would slow some too
On your sleeve

You lie in bed
The light on
The sounds of the cold air
Through a hole in the wall
Making appearances in the kitchen

Sure the animal means something
More than a dead thing in the tub

Sure someone is in the dark
In the room you didn't check
Before returning to bed

You are not allowed to be scared
You have to get up and check the dark house
Yourself

You're fighting air
There's nothing there

And back in bed
The same cold wind rumbles

The animal will be there
In the morning
A dried out mess smelling
Of lemon cleaning spray and urea
For now you calm yourself
With the blue light
To forget you have no power

LA FLEUVE

Down to Sugar Beach
summers ago that afternoon
eating strawberries and running
our feet through the sand.
Dunked in the teacup
ourselves and the rest of Montreal's
July folk yearning for a wind
in the lake beside the casino
walking through the Chinese gardens
past the Ontario pavilion.
Outside your home
I said the bike ride back
was good
you said tiring.

TRANQUILIZER

He says
his thinking
is broken.

I see
maybe foggy
pieces not fitting
on a foggy hill,

but he runs those
hill paths
to their utter end
slapping his body
into glass doors.
He keeps hitting.

He is sitting in the chair
crying in his hands.

I am looking out the window
at the red hibiscus
slouching in the rain.

No one can hear us.
The neighbors can't hear us
under the downpour.

Water is lapping at the front door
and I let the window drops
pool in my hand.

HEPATITIS

Funerary deity
growing large
on the windowsill.

Inflamed sugar spots.
Liver
living in the air —

four days
in bristles.

Not sick
from you
but the thought of you.

BREAKING AND ENTERING

Never into a house that isn't my own
Never in a far muskeg
Never past the pink concrete altar where roasted the Christmas pig
Never under a hush, slipping off my shoes, letting you check
        the door first
Never with people practicing dreams upstairs
There was a slight tree in the yard lit with sleeping birds
Whispering you owned nothing
O stricken crossing of the bed O great herons
Still on the asphalt there are small fires burning
We can see their fervor in the winter cattails
The canals are low tonight
On the grass beside the house we watched the stars
Blazing mouthful of minor constellations
Breathing in dusty swamp gas
Still and greasy as two gators
Not that it was empty or cold
Not that we found our heady air elsewhere
Not that I was square
But that wilderness vibrated higher and louder than we knew
It shook us and sent us shivering apart
I understood the feeling just miles later
Avoiding U-turns on drained land
Driving lost on turnpike mazes
Too close to the wild, that was what it was

HOME VIDEOS

Mom's murmured morning
incantations to her two messy love birds
the year I moved away.
Ferdinand and Ella growing,
birthing eggs, and forcing
digested millet pods and lettuce
into their own lavender babies,
their inbred, squawking, tulip buds.
I watch them grow in fast-forward
from the small foldable side monitor.
Their grassy nest and the snow
piled up to the windows, the salmon
pink on the walls, all wound
in the camera's spool. That house
we left years ago looped over too.
I pause the tape on a blurry baby bird
eating something green
out of my mother's hand,
and on her lips I can see
the psalm she sings
them as they feed.

MUNCHAUSEN BY PROXY

1.
Oh the many ways
I could die!
The Honey!
The Honey!
The Sea! Love
is a sea in me.
He swims about it
in himself
in me swims
about it
in the tinder house
with the altar
pan-frying robins' eggs.
The sickness has moved
between my ears
and I'm glad.
The house is quiet now
and dark as always.
I've lain wrapped here
a thick Christmas pig
pressed the silver spider
into the wall
and my finger
came away clean.
The house
as a swamp
outside
could be robin's egg blue.
Pussy could be in the grass—
was that her scratching at the wire?
I can't tell anymore, everything's gone.

I can still hear mongrel
coughing at me through the wood.
Will someone shoot
that dog?
If I stop breathing will he know?
Silence like a gunblast,
the neighbors gathering, knowing
they'd bring crowbars, rip
where the door used to be
and walk into my garden
sprouting through the floor.
Pools of water lettuce
in the bath
climbing aster and dog fennel
in doorways
glasswort turning red
in the dark
a green blooming
chalk line in the air
that space between
my neck and shoulder
my arm and chest
pierced by Spanish bayonets.

2.
In the tinder house
drinking blue
the sickness
between my ears
quiet now
dark as always
in the wall.

My rising humors
are imbalanced.
I've lost my choler
for a wet sanguinity
that comes upon me
sweetly, in the middle
of traffic, at the copyist's,
while I'm boxing.
I'm fighting air
there's nothing there.
okay cool
no
smoking love pony

3.
In the tinder house
drinking robin's eggs.
In the flight path
moon rising like a plane.
In the grass
like a cat
blue
at her fertility.
The sickness has moved
the forgiveness
unsure in me.
Over the living
room the pink book
light in my hands
reading the female saints
wrapped thick pig
pressed silver
to the wall.
The swamp inside
my head this time
the birds
nesting
in the marsh.
I'm shooting full rounds
into the mongrel water.
Are you still under there?

4.
I go inside
my head
for a second
and there is
a different taste
between
my teeth
how did mint get there?
In big bushes
from our dinner plates
it's here now
in my molars
like a licorice seed.
If I don't
breathe a
certain way
the black
bird flies
over
beat beat
my head
then
coughs come
angled in my lungs.
I taste blood.
I heave
and seize
my organs
bellow with
a lost fire
ringing

my ribs
birds roost
with each coo
I bring up
green feathers
I am
bleeding now
breathing
shallow scoops
the croupe calms
my love
is full of sleep
and feels
good in my hand.

5.
The saint found fire
most places.
Clustered caviar
on the river
or spiraling
upward over the bridge
many loud noises
sometimes
the fire was purple
or green
and it fell golden
over the city.

By the eucalyptus forest
they are hosing
fragrant autumn
out of the trees
seed pods popping
like old stars in the heat.

6.
The books here are covered with velvet.
The ceiling is stamped with rings.

At this hour the termites
shed their wings in small bonfires.
Pyres in the kitchen sink.
The air is cold and stale
from the box.
No-seeums thick
and well fed.

Cars
and bodies
and
Jesus in the ocean.

We're trying to get deeper
where it's cooler
and the cars
keep passing through us
the road is moving
over the waves.

The saint
looks so tired.
He's been hanging
there forever.
Isn't he cold
looking into the
pond below

where the goldfish
grow on host scraps
and some days
are picked out
of the water
gasping and flailing
in the air.

7.
Everyone is running
from the water
wet and crying
with the wind
at their backs.
I'm not afraid
anymore
I want to go next.
I bite the arm
and spit out the blood.
If the cup
in my chest dripped
over I'd go
but it's crystal
and busy,
other side of the city
away from the salt,
in the swamp.
Love is a gold cup
in the chest
filling with drips.
My love-cup!
My horse! My wolf
in the flesh!
I've been at the water
all this time
and I haven't gone in!
The Swim! The Swim!
I haven't gone in!

8.
The sickness in the pool
gets between my ears
and I'm glad.

Come over now
bring your
burnt lips to the candle
and blow it out.
No love.
Dark as always
I've lain here pressed silver
into my finger
came away clean.
Outside could be robin's egg.
Pussy could be in the grass,
was that her scratching at the wire?
I can't tell anymore, everything's gone.

The saints in the road took it.
They are piling it all under the saints.
It's quiet on the road.
They closed it for the pyre.
Children lie in the mongrel grass
under a shady tree
and wait.

Will someone light
that fire?
If they stop breathing will we know?
And walk into the garden

sprouting through the floor
smoke on our hair
choking the plants
singing honey up from the walls
thinking on our sins
stacked in the bathtub
precarious and wet
glittering like Spanish bayonets.

SURPRISING ANIMALS

Who was that animal
yelling *Woman!* into my thighs?
Shirtless and proud, its striped heart
beat soundless rounds all night
so I couldn't sleep and gazed jealous
as it mouth-breathed in dreams
holding my hands, my belly, my breast,
until finally I woke it from its rest.

We must've looked like a couple
of night bears swaggering with heat,
reminders of claws and padded feet,
furry confetti falling outside the window,
walls holding marks from our hands
and teeth, hibernating under rocky sheets.

When we needed to we wandered
up to the roof of a parking garage
and climbed in cars, the emergency brake
between us, the moon turning orange
overhead, herons skimming
the lake for pears and fish
and women calling into dark yards
after loose dogs and children.

MARCH STORM

You told me to call into your radio
to get us tickets to the St. Patty's show.
Snow like cereal around us. Sky a spilled bowl.
Standing in the milk I chugged my last Keystone.

After I bought frozen macaroni and more beers,
you passed out on my couch
and my roommate said you were *My Man*.
I said *I doubt it* and left the noodles on your dormant belly.

Out in the parking lot below my room
the cars were like cake decorations
and no one climbed the stairs to my window.

RED, WHITE, AND BLUE

It's overcast
and we pass
a drift of them,
men in hip waders,
deep denim blue.

the tall dark and new
the red white and blue

Driving by we see
flashes of indigo
and onionskin
flaxy and deep
in the current
black where the water,
thrashing at
the warm night,
leapt out of itself.

Earlier that day,
our work clothes dripped
tradition like iron into the dirt.

WILDWIFE

I'm a little slow
just getting it now
that I was in Cali six months ago
camped in a parking lot
in the middle of a wind storm
some teens burning wood
a few cars down.
Finally I gave up and folded the tent
in the loud, ashy wind
into the trunk full of sand,
crawled into the car to sleep
wrapped in all the clothes I had.
The next morning was my first
surf lesson. I didn't know
it wasn't normal
for your instructor
to step into the outdoor shower
and help you take off your wetsuit
after holding your ass in the waves
and telling you the story
of how a seal
crazy from summer algae
jumped onto his back
and squeezed his sides.
I think it was a compliment,
he told me. *That bull*
wanted to make me his wife.

HEPATITIS

White noise
to me.

Peacocks scream in another yard,
pecking their reflections
in the hubcaps of cars.

Her madness
the sound of water
boiling unchecked.

THE NIGHT MY STARTER DIED IN WYNWOOD

There are people dancing
on top of ice cream trucks
and horses in the street.
Two girls in silver give me a Red Bull.
I drink it sweet waiting for Triple A.
My car unresponsive in the heat
of Art Basel Weekend, the dog tinkering
at my feet, a graffiti artist from Chicago
cuffed across the street.
Are you in a safe place?
AAA asks. *Kinda*, I bleat.

Somehow the tow finds me crosshatched
between new galleries and body shops.
Blocking the entire road with his truck,
my driver tells me nothing
is impossible, kicks my car into neutral
and chains up my little hatchback
as shuttles of party people pile in front
and behind him—coked-out Bluechip art
snobs and locals looking for free booze—
honking and reversing into alleys.

Perched in the cab,
we barrel through Midtown
sending jaywalkers sprinting
to the curb, talking about why
you didn't pick me up tonight.

When I get home I keep thinking.
I don't call you but suspect
you'll want to hear

about the horses and the tow.
You're caffeinated too and
familiar with the dark places
a hit of Taurine can fly a person
that fifth of the month, moon
hanging like a heavy breast,
Suicide Girls trolling your rest,
mouth full of oxtail and oiled bread,
saying you're already here,
in my computer, in my bed.

MIAMI AS LOVER

All through this black moon
night, I've been woken by offers of sex
and the weeping chorus of balcony dogs.
I ask you to turn on the fan, to lift off the duvet,
but you refuse, telling me the names of your girlfriends
and all the books you've read lately.

I put on your shearling coat and empty its pockets.
I pummel you with mitten fists
until you cry out that you invented ironic,
before the Internet, you invented it!
I jump on you again.
I'm going to marry an American,
I tell you, *but it won't be you.*

RED EYE

This red eye
over America
our little shadow
running into things below
typeset farmlands
peach velvet hills
this mother rock
all sharp and deep.
There was just land
a long time.
I was a city girl
in too much space,
had the stolen sheep, o sleep,
and forgot my body.

For a while yellow cities
buzzing under the wing outside,
maybe Eugene, maybe Laramie,
a half circle doming the lights,
small thinnings in the greater cloth
where the towns get through.

Couldn't bring you up here
but wanted to—
wormholes, inverted whirlpools—
maybe on piggyback.

How can I write this?
Do I have no reverence?
We shake through the morning
fuzz cover.
Angels on the windshield,
on the wings.

SANDY

There are horses dancing in the river,
there is fire burning through the flood.
Down under the Manhattan Bridge
Jane's Carousel is in the East River.
Her fair bulbs the only light between us
and the mainland since the island
lost its distinction from ocean or night.
Miles downwind, your Atlantic gale
chips away at Jersey's neon shore-gem.
We are precarious and blind-spotted.
Breezy Point is still smoking days later.
Its salty blister draining into the sea.

FIRST TATTOO

Dreamed I was walking in waist-deep water.
Woke up anxious I'd ruined the tattoo.
Woke up and already regretted it.

We were all brothers and sisters that night,
comparing our machetes, our cockroaches,
our dominoes, our diamonds, bleeding
in the barroom lobby and our plastic wrap,
stepping out into the strip mall parking lot
to get in cars and push through yellow lights,
gold chains swinging from the rear-view mirror,
our bald tires salty, the sea rising from the sewer.

SEA LIGHTNING

Underneath us a silver cobra
coiled and bobbed in the rocks,
flagging the oncoming tide
like clusters of hard roe
in standing water.

We sit under the sea grapes,
ants pulling their dead over our arms.

White bay.
Plastic sails.
We walk with lemons in our teeth.
I keep looking back
at the three grey pyres
of ponderosa green
molting their heat
over the sea.

Purple night
here too.

The saint and I
ran through the fields
and flirted with the foggy edges
of the trees.

That evening we walked to the cabin,
terror-lost in the dark and
suffocating on our blindness.

THE BLUE MILK BOY OF AVEYRON

Milk from the big blue. Oh Dieu.
Oh Dieu of milk in the reaching place.
Every reach milky. Hot danger
in the reaching place. Fast reaches
in the milk. Things get fast as I get full.
The reaches are different
when the big blue is different.
The big blue. Oh Dieu.
The multitudes say that and point up.
Oh Dieu. They point at milk
in their strange reach and say milk.
I see milk in Mon Dieu.
The multitudes point to a little clawed
and say it again. Oh Dieu.
Milk really is everywhere. Milk on clawed
in the reaches. Milk on me in my hole.
Milk on the dwellers.
Heat on the milk making it blue.
I show them I know Mon Dieu.
I point and yell it. I move to the reaches
and sit in the milk, reaching big blue.

HOW TO GET THE GHOST
OUT OF THE POOL

Dead heat boiled the water alive that summer.
Even the cement greened over with carpetgrass
and sedge. The fountain dribbled dutifully on,
spitting and gurgling its turgid mouthful
back into the cyano pool where tadpoles
birthed themselves in sun.

The water surged especially at night.
Surface roiling, doubling.
Chloro tones caught in the oily water
and wavered in the overhanging willows.
The pool was still lit, it cast algae shadows
over the tops of the animary sprouts
beside the house, those hedges of cowthistle,
lambsquarters and pigweed guarding the sink.

There was something more in the water.
The dogs avoided it, so did the birds.

When the new family moved in
they razed the backyard field.
Dandelion heads ringed with white
blood were gathered into brown bags
and sat at the curb. The pool was next.

They dragged it clean of the swollen berries
and banana leaves, scattering the sediment
around the trimmed willow.
The homogenous water lay green
in the autumn chill and they shocked it
with chlorine, revealing new spots in the jellybean,

bleaching the quilled fur of the raccoon
bloated in a curve under the diving board.
When they lifted it out, tugging on their net,
the smell hung like a haunt over the pool.

The animal was long ago wrapped
in bags and buried out beyond the willow
where it wouldn't affect the well,
but even now, though the pool was drained
and as irises root over its nitrous decay,
the smell of the animal, not unpleasant,
like crabapples rotting in the sun,
remains, ghosting over their barbeques,
goosebumping women's thighs between
the plastic lawn chair ribbons, speaking
of a shyer season, when sun grew hesitant
bundles of wheat and grass against the bricks.

LA DELUGE

A flood rose,
lifted us off our feet.
The earth's watery eye
blinking us back quite easily,
like the eight jaybirds
shake their powdered wings.

We the bait ball split by tuna.
The green flow and the ferrous bodies.
The silver fish and their soundless fight.

In the late half-light, we caught
their yellow underbellies in flight.
It was quiet,
like a barracuda and a silver net.

PARANOID POEM

Hammer is within reach
when I finally fall asleep
on the couch by the door
with the AC off
so I can hear better.
Through the peep-hole
shadows were people,
then they were gone.
I triple-check the locks
and review
the ports of entry:
water, air, road.

SELFIES

I am a birthday cake bear.
I am a plush wooly child.
I am icing the edge
of the false sky and the wild.

The northern noon
carries the church bells
and the palm starving at the glass
in its thin arms.
From its spot in the room
it sings in a soft voice
about spring, about worms,
about braided bread on the windowsill.

It is the Middle Ages
behind me.
Melancholic
greyhounds, yellow
songbirds and enormous fish
all equalized in a 2-D berry field.
Cherries and blue plums.
The small yellow blossoms
of the chicory root.
Medieval edelweiss
in a flattened forest plane.
Everything is baroque
about the Middle Ages.

My furniture doesn't have boundary issues.
My furniture isn't overwrought in afternoon light.
My furniture doesn't open the window onto
purple roses and a silver spruce.
Not sure how my mental health is.
Alright I guess. Didn't look
up much but here are my eyes.

Oh, the shoes are
black and clean
like guns hanging from my knees,
my legs like delicious braided loaves
you might find
by a window growing old.

The bees, the bear,
the trees,
the only meaty one
surviving the freeze.

My floor is yellow.
Our roof is fragrant and autumn.
Celebrate me on this brown table.
I am the cake and the party.

NOTES

"Selfies" is after Iiu Susiraja.

"Ritual Union" is after Little Dragon and Sylvia Plath.

"Monster" is after Aileen Wuoronos.

"Bull Among the Narcissi" is after Sylvia Plath and Ocean Vuong.

"Little Fugue State" is after Sylvia Plath.

"Wash Bucket," "Domestic Disturbance," "They Took Their Time," "Squalor," and "The Ottawa Valley" are partial Golden Shovels after Yusef Komunyakaa's "Yellowjackets," "Urban Renewal," "Yellow Dog Cafe," and "A Good Memory," respectively. The Golden Shovel is a form invented by Terrance Hayes.

"They found the boy" is after a painting of the same title by Andrea Joyce Heimer. The first six lines of the poem are from her painting.

"Broken Air Conditioner Poems" is after Colossians 2:9, Daniel 12:1, and Revelation 11:15.

"On MC Hammer's Birthday" is after Frank O'Hara.

"The Blue Milk Boy of Aveyron": Victor of Aveyron was a feral child found in the French woods in 1800. The only phrases he learned were "Oh Dieu" and "Lait"—or "Oh God" and "Milk."

"Munchausen by Proxy" is after Hector Veil Temperly's "Hospital Brittanico" and inspired by Sue Montoya's photography.

ABOUT THE AUTHOR

Annik Adey-Babinski grew up in Ottawa, Canada. She has received fellowships from the Banff Center and The John S. and James L. Knight Foundation. Her poetry has appeared in *Forklift*, *Ohio*, *Prelude*, and the *Best New Poets* series. Her poems were also published in the Jai-Alai Books anthology *Eight Miami Poets*. She is a technical writer in Miami, Florida.

ABOUT THE ARTIST

Sue Montoya is an artist based in Miami and Gainesville. She received a BFA in Visual Arts from New World School of the Arts in 2014. Much of her work draws on geology, architecture, and land use to document the rapidly changing landscape of Florida. When she is not taking photographs, she is sipping *cafecitos* at her favorite Hialeah haunts.

OTHER WORD WORKS BOOKS

Karren L. Alenier, *Wandering on the Outside*
Karren L. Alenier, ed., *Whose Woods These Are*
Christopher Bursk, ed., *Cool Fire*
Barbara Goldberg, *Berta Broadfoot and Pepin the Short*
Frannie Lindsay, *If Mercy*
Elaine Magarrell, *The Madness of Chefs*
Marilyn McCabe, *Glass Factory*
Ann Pelletier, *Letter That Never*
Ayaz Pirani, *Happy You Are Here*
W.T. Pfefferle, *My Coolest Shirt*
Jacklyn Potter, Dwaine Rieves, Gary Stein, eds.,
Cabin Fever: Poets at Joaquin Miller's Cabin
Robert Sargent, *Aspects of a Southern Story*
       & *A Woman from Memphis*
Fritz Ward, *Tsunami Diorama*
Amber West, *Hen & God*
Nancy White, ed., *Word for Word*

INTERNATIONAL EDITIONS

Kajal Ahmad (Alana Marie Levinson-LaBrosse, Mewan Nahro
Said Sofi, and Darya Abdul-Karim Ali Najin, trans., with
Barbara Goldberg), *Handful of Salt*
Keyne Cheshire (trans.), *Murder at Jagged Rock: A Tragedy by
Sophocles*
Jean Cocteau (Mary-Sherman Willis, trans.), *Grace Notes*
Yoko Danno & James C. Hopkins, *The Blue Door*
Moshe Dor, Barbara Goldberg, Giora Leshem, eds.,
The Stones Remember: Native Israeli Poets
Moshe Dor (Barbara Goldberg, trans.), *Scorched by the Sun*
Lee Sang (Myong-Hee Kim, trans.), *Crow's Eye View: The Infamy
of Lee Sang, Korean Poet*
Vladimir Levchev (Henry Taylor, trans.), *Black Book of the
Endangered Species*

The Washington Prize

Nathalie F. Anderson, *Following Fred Astaire*, 1998

Michael Atkinson, *One Hundred Children Waiting for a Train*, 2001

Molly Bashaw, *The Whole Field Still Moving Inside It*, 2013

Carrie Bennett, *biography of water*, 2004

Peter Blair, *Last Heat*, 1999

John Bradley, *Love-in-Idleness: The Poetry of Roberto Zingarello*, 1995, 2nd edition 2014

Christopher Bursk, *The Way Water Rubs Stone*, 1988

Richard Carr, *Ace*, 2008

Jamison Crabtree, *Rel[AM]ent*, 2014

Jessica Cuello, *Hunt*, 2016

B. K. Fischer, *St. Rage's Vault*, 2012

Linda Lee Harper, *Toward Desire*, 1995

Ann Rae Jonas, *A Diamond Is Hard But Not Tough*, 1997

Frannie Lindsay, *Mayweed*, 2009

Richard Lyons, *Fleur Carnivore*, 2005

Elaine Magarrell, *Blameless Lives*, 1991

Fred Marchant, *Tipping Point*, 1993

Ron Mohring, *Survivable World*, 2003

Barbara Moore, *Farewell to the Body*, 1990

Brad Richard, *Motion Studies*, 2010

Jay Rogoff, *The Cutoff*, 1994

Prartho Sereno, *Call from Paris*, 2007, 2nd edition 2013

Enid Shomer, *Stalking the Florida Panther*, 1987

John Surowiecki, *The Hat City After Men Stopped Wearing Hats*, 2006

Miles Waggener, *Phoenix Suites*, 2002

Charlotte Warren, *Gandhi's Lap*, 2000

Mike White, *How to Make a Bird with Two Hands*, 2011

Nancy White, *Sun, Moon, Salt*, 1992, 2nd edition 2010

George Young, *Spinoza's Mouse*, 1996

THE HILARY THAM CAPITAL COLLECTION

Nathalie Anderson, *Stain*
Mel Belin, *Flesh That Was Chrysalis*
Carrie Bennett, *The Land Is a Painted Thing*
Doris Brody, *Judging the Distance*
Sarah Browning, *Whiskey in the Garden of Eden*
Grace Cavalieri, *Pinecrest Rest Haven*
Cheryl Clarke, *By My Precise Haircut*
Christopher Conlon, *Gilbert and Garbo in Love*
      & Mary Falls: Requiem for Mrs. Surratt
Donna Denizé, *Broken like Job*
W. Perry Epes, *Nothing Happened*
David Eye, *Seed*
Bernadette Geyer, *The Scabbard of Her Throat*
Barbara G. S. Hagerty, *Twinzilla*
James Hopkins, *Eight Pale Women*
Brandon Johnson, *Love's Skin*
Marilyn McCabe, *Perpetual Motion*
Judith McCombs, *The Habit of Fire*
James McEwen, *Snake Country*
Miles David Moore, *The Bears of Paris*
      & Rollercoaster
Kathi Morrison-Taylor, *By the Nest*
Tera Vale Ragan, *Reading the Ground*
Michael Shaffner, *The Good Opinion of Squirrels*
Maria Terrone, *The Bodies We Were Loaned*
Hilary Tham, *Bad Names for Women*
      & Counting
Barbara Louise Ungar, *Charlotte Brontë, You Ruined My Life*
      & Immortal Medusa
Jonathan Vaile, *Blue Cowboy*
Rosemary Winslow, *Green Bodies*
Michele Wolf, *Immersion*
Joe Zealberg, *Covalence*

THE TENTH GATE PRIZE

Jennifer Barber, *Works on Paper*, 2015
Roger Sedarat, *Haji as Puppet*, 2016
Lisa Sewell, *Impossible Object*, 2014

www.ingramcontent.com/pod-product-compliance
Lightning Source LLC
Chambersburg PA
CBHW030854090426
42737CB00009B/1225